Bill Steinkraus

Joan Gold

George Hills

S. Hall

Graham Mancinelli

May Bay

David Brown

Anna Clement

FiLatov

Bay Lane

Chammartin

Anne Townsend.

Liselott Linsenhoff

George H. Morris

Willi White

The Equestrian World

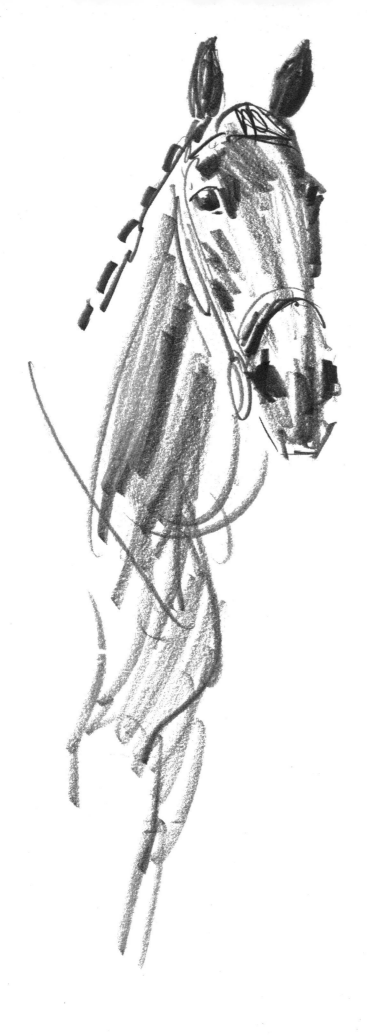

FRONTISPIECE *The United States
Equestrian Team, Dublin 1962*

The Equestrian World

seen by

Keith Money

FRANKLIN WATTS INC.

BOOK DESIGNED BY KEITH MONEY

Library of congress catalog card number 64–11920

First American Publication 1963
by FRANKLIN WATTS INC.
575 Lexington Avenue, New York.
© *Keith Money 1963*
Composed in Plantin and Printed in the Netherlands
by L. Van Leer and Co. N.V.

for PAT SMYTHE

as a token salute to her unique
career, and in recognition of
the key part she has played in
helping to popularize showjumping, far beyond her home
shores

6

FOREWORD BY

BILL STEINKRAUS

I have been advised, by strangers passing through, that the equestrian world seems to outsiders a foreign place indeed, full of strange sights and sounds, inhabited by assorted eccentric people most variously and curiously attired, and ruled by four-legged creatures ironically described as 'noble servants.' On the other hand, a younger generation of visitors seems to find it less forbidding—for to many children, the equestrian world seems almost magical, so full of excitement and enchantment that their parents can finally convey them away from it only forcibly, if at all.

It would be convenient to say that the truth lies somewhere between these two views, but in fact, I think that both are encompassed by it; for the equestrian world seems to me an almost perfect microcosm in which the most widely divergent elements are somehow bound together by their common interest in the horse. The prince and the pauper, the rich man, beggar man and thief are all represented in the equestrian world, often in a most revealing light—and the juxtaposition is no less plausible there than in 'real life.' It is not easy to convey the texture of so rich a fabric between the covers of a book. Many of the travel books that seek to introduce the visitor to a world that is foreign to him restrict themselves to portraying, very selectively, an idealized reflection of what is *there;* we are usually shown only sunny skies, the smiling faces, and the architectural glories unmarred by pedestrians (presumably at five o'clock in the morning).

Keith Money has set himself the more difficult task, it seems to me, of communicating what it is *like* to *be* there. Thus, while his riders are *some-*

times triumphant, and his horses *sometimes* make a perfect bascule, his riders are also sometimes alone and wet and tired, and his horses sometimes 'hang their knees.' Nor has he forgotten that horses have grooms, who must be up early and finish late even when the performance was one the public scarcely noticed and the rider would prefer to forget. Even beyond this, his perceptive eye and sensitive hand have often succeeded in capturing the essence as well as the literal outline of many of the scenes that are most characteristic of the equestrian world I know—and he has captured much of their subtler beauty, too.

For those who have never lost their sense of enchantment with the equestrian world—and I am one of them, Keith Money's present book provides a delightful vehicle to transport us vicariously from our easy chair back into a world we love. But I shall be surprised if it does not serve also as a visa that will permit a new group of travellers to penetrate the borders of that extraordinary domain that is The Equestrian World.

Bill Steinkraus

Since the time when chisel was first set to stone to commemorate them, Man and the Horse have striven together, in the exultant labours of victory and the agonies of defeat. Their paths have crossed and their destinies intermingled within the tangle of history to such an extent that of all creatures non-human, it is the Horse that has most moulded our ancestors' lives. Great men who are also humble men have seen in the Horse a mirror of all they would wish to retain in human form: strength concealed in graceful movement; symmetry of shape; courage, nobility and pride. Men lacking in all these attributes have sought to rob the Horse of his own natural dignity in humiliating circumstances, exploiting the Horse's great strength, abusing his patience and demanding loyalty when they themselves have none.

Horses are not all virtuous, but equine frailties often have their beginnings in the first encounters with Man, and if we can only remember that 'to err is human,' then we may be on the way to educating ourselves in our attempts to 'educate' the Horse. If the dust of battles has settled, the blood dried, and the neighing of horses has been replaced in recent times by the unmerciful din of machinery, we can at least be thankful that the Horse has remained with us in a variety of roles. In many parts of the world he is still indispensable. To some people he will be a curiosity, misunderstood or ignored, but to others he will in all probability be well established in the order of activities on this earth. If he is not at work in the fields or on the racecourse, he will certainly be the partner in numerous sports and pastimes.

A poor rider is a sorry sight; a harsh rider is an ugly sight; but a good rider, in tune with his horse, can rise to the heights, and in the process provide himself with the subtle elation of the spirit that arrives after mind and body have achieved that rare and perfect co-ordination. His pleasure will be magnified by the partnership, and for those watching, the spectacle will have them wholly involved. Partisanship is an obvious facet of international competitions, and it would be a poor person who did not exult in his teams' victories and feel a tinge of sadness at their defeats. Again, in the Olympic Games, when the nations of the world display their powers unarmed, of all the animals it is only the Horse that finds a part to play in this human concourse. For the span of each Olympiad, horses and riders around the world are toiling in their separate countries, equipping themselves for those relatively brief moments at each Olympic Games. The Equestrian Games are the flowering of these labours; sometimes the bloom is bright and magnificent; sometimes it is destined to wither prematurely; but always, it is drama on a scale we cannot witness again until another four years have passed.

Rome, in the late summer of 1960, saw the story repeated. The struggles, triumphs and disasters unfolded again, culminating in that long, exhausting day—the final day of the Games—when 100,000 people packed themselves into the vast Stadio Olimpico to witness eighteen teams compete for the Nations Grand Prix; gold medals and glory at one end of the scale and bitter humiliation at the other end. Often throughout the week, during the Three-Day Event and the Individual Showjumping Event, the courses had proved to be far beyond the capabilities of a great number of competitors. In the Nations' competition, too, the suicidal courage of many men and horses was not always enough to extricate them from disaster. Watching those solitary contenders—sometimes one's personal friends—dwarfed in the midst of that fantastic and relentless crowd, one had the chilling experience of sensing what the atmosphere must have been like on those similar occasions in the Rome of earlier centuries. If this could be sensed from the Gallery, what tumult and numbness must have been lurking in the minds of those who were the object of such concentrated attention? For them, the arena at Rome was probably the loneliest spot they will ever have to face in all their lives.

MEMORIES OF
THE ROME OLYMPICS

Some flew in out of the echoing blue skies above the city; others convoyed for days and nights by road. Whatever the method of travel, men and horses streamed into Rome for the acting out of their hopes and fears of months past. The Eternal City was its usual hot, colourful self, caught up in the sense of occasion but not altogether sure how to express itself. The overlay of importance disturbed the panache of the city, but from the outskirts, until one caught sight of the ranks of flagpoles, there was no hint of what was afoot. Tired and dusty foreign drivers pressed on the accelerator over the last endless miles approaching Rome, with the ruler-straight ribbon of brown road piercing the heat haze in the distance. Slowly, the city of Rome caught them into its encircling vortex of roads, drawing them inwards and digesting them, while drivers strained and squinted at the rash of lemon-yellow directional markers that pointed back upon one another in bright confusion, swivelling at the slightest touch of wind or prankish fingers. Immaculate traffic policemen were not beguiled by pleas of help. The white batons continued to flash imperiously; always onwards. Dusty horse-boxes were engulfed in the hoard of waspish Lambrettas and svelte Alfa Romeos that jostled impatiently behind the batons, like horses at a starting gate.

Show-jumpers and dressage horses were to be billeted at the Villa Glori Stables.

"Villa Glori ?"

The epaulettes only shrugged fractionally in reply. No one appeared to know, and no one was pleased that their ignorance should be put to the test. Each personality retreated behind the universal facade of sun-glasses, and one's own blank look was reflected back impassively. Quite suddenly, and quite by chance, the haven was discovered. In the gateway there were sentries that betrayed a flicker of recognition. Even the trolley cars slowed down, as if expecting the horse-boxes themselves to shie out into the centre of the tree-dappled road.

From the encircling retreat of the Villa Glori Stables, Rome at night took on a leisurely, detached atmosphere. The warm, enervating night air blanketed the city, leaving the acacia leaves hanging listless and still, silhouetted against the indigo sky and in sharper relief, against the lurid tinge of pink and green lights that rinsed into the darkness. The stars hung almost unblinking, aloof from the flashing lights of aeroplanes and the hastening spot of a solitary satellite which plunged across their formal patterns like a gatecrasher at a party. In this relatively peaceful retreat, the night sounds of the city were filtered, and cars seldom heard. Only the gunfire and staccato chatter from the television set under the vine-draped overhang of the stable yard, and the dynamic whine of Viscounts overhead, intruded upon the stillness. The thud of a horse kicking against a stable door and the occasional clink of a bucket came as distant punctuations. This was the grooms' world, divided by a road and a prison-camp barrier of wire mesh from the Olympic Village, where the riders lodged.

The jump from the Mexican-style aura of the Stables to the concrete and polished granite of the Village was architecturally enormous. Laced with miniature streets and avenues, the vast apartments hovered on stilts, each providing underneath a cool, colonnaded oasis of shade. Everything was barely finished; the grass in the dividing plots was lank and sparse from fresh sowing. The colour came not from the surroundings, which were blanched by the sun, but from the exotic, multi-coloured casual garb of the inhabitants as they promenaded about their miniature city. Within the polished simplicity of the buildings (later to be used as normal city apartments), the personalities of the competitors transformed each into an untidy form of high school. Disordered bed-

clothes, wet bathing suits hanging on the window-ledges, scattered clothes, empty coat-hangers, bottles of soft drinks, photographs and newspaper cuttings provided the clutter for every room. Spurs and riding boots seemed to tangle a shade incongruously with track shoes and zip-suits. Team managers found their tiny offices crammed with cartons of Lucozade, packets of glucose tablets, stacks of records overprinted with Coca-Cola advertising, glossy pamphlets on the tourist's city of Rome. Everything free. The shops below sold their wares, but the cafeterias of each nation provided a rich bonus as well as the sumptuous choice of meals. Choice fruit piled in abundance; staff hands constantly refilled the giant refrigerators with fruit juices, beverages and milk. Evenings in the Village were more cosmopolitan. The shops remained open; there was laughter on the night air; and in the great segments of shadow under each building the flickering eye of a television camera acted out its canned drama to a sparse audience—often only a couple of bored guards, unless there happened to be a replay of highlights of the day in the main stadium. Then, curious athletes sat forward and watched those vividly recent events from the anonymity of a deck-chair.

Late at night, the Three-Day Event riders stumbled in, dust-caked and weary from their training efforts in the arid plateau 2,000 feet up in the mountains behind Rome. In this dust-bedevilled area where water was at a premium and had to be stored in canvas tanks, there were none of the facilities that made life easier for the showjumpers and dressage horses quartered at the Villa Glori, where one of the early morning sounds was the swoosh of the water-cart on its routine dust-laying mission. The drive to the Three-Day Event headquarters at Pratoni del Vivaro was a magnificent one scenically, but to those horsemen who had to make the eighteen-mile journey to the Olympic Village two and three times a day, it became another endurance test. The sun-baked ground gave team veterinary surgeons their problems, as horse after horse was trotted out anxiously for their inspection.

Mercifully, an intimidating thunderstorm cracked overhead before the events began. For hours it raged with true pagan ferocity, splitting the leaden air with terrifying crumps of thunder that sent the horses recoiling wide-eyed in their boxes. The rain fell with bullet strength, battering the vine leaves and cascading in great curtains from the gutters and eaves. "Certainly the worst for many years," nodded the locals when it was over and the whole of the Stable courtyard was a solid lake of some depth. Incredibly, the water-cart was needed for its dust-laying mission again the following day, but at Pratoni, the rain had drawn the worst sting from the ground. Only the awesome fences retained their real harshness. Most memories of Rome in 1960 will be clouded by the grim struggles these courses provoked. When it was all over there was a sense of depression. In the northern mountain passes, the chill mists of autumn were already creeping among the dark pine trees, and the ice sliding from the wet slates of the frontier outposts echoed behind us as we headed homeward.

15

STADIO
OLIMPICO
ROME
1960

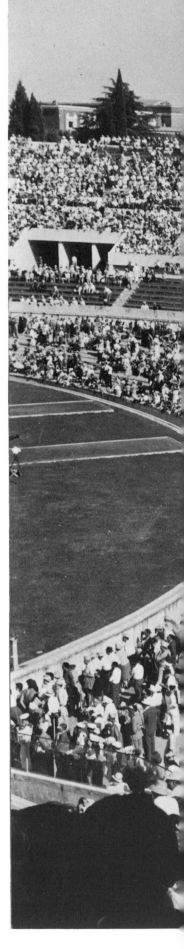

The air sings with heat under an azure sky. Ice-cream vendors chant incessantly as 100,000 spectators converge for the final day of the 1960 Olympics. Bright yellow paper hats dot the vast crowd, there to witness what proves to be an almost gladiatorial contest between the finest riders that each nation can produce as a team, over a course that finds many combinations of horse and rider unequal to the task. The sky pales to saffron and dusk approaches before the victorious German team finally takes its place of honour in the centre of the darkening arena.

Germany's unbeatably consistent Olympic team: Hans Günter Winkler, Alwin Schockemöhle and Fritz Thiedemann

What of the backroom boys, whose loyalties and labours are responsible for the well-being of each horse? The horse at the end of the line has received just as much devotion and care as the animal that stands in the winner's position. The groom's world is a world of early morning's labour that often continues far into the night. Their charges demand attention pleasantly but incessantly; their employers likewise—sometimes forgetting the pleasantness. Always, the glamour by-passes them; the glory only reflected. The world of the Groom is a domain where loyalty is the keyword and good humour a prized asset—a world of considerable complexity with a code of its own.

For all its labours, grooming can have its compensations when the charges are international, and although the travel itself may at times be uncomfortable, there are rare opportunities to glimpse new sights during off-duty moments. For the Americans in particular, air transport is an everyday occurrence, and the elaborate and immaculate headquarters they set up at every stop are worth a special visit.

The Individual event for showjumpers takes place in mid-week at the famous Piazza di Siena in the Borghese Gardens. The first rider is due to start at 7 A.M., at a time when the dew is still wet upon the grass and the morning sun only just glinting through the cypresses and umbrella pines. Individual tension is all too plainly evident behind the falsely jocular remarks. After perhaps four years of intensive work with this moment as its objective, the grooms now have a brief half-hour of comparative relaxation, when they can stand on the wall of the grounds and observe the first few competitors before disappearing to see their own charges safely into the ring. Here, Hans Günter Winkler strides off to do battle, while his countryman, Alwin Schockemöhle, accepts good wishes from the American groom Jack Kettering.

Towards that brief twelve minutes under the judges' eyes, dressage riders continue their assiduous training in Rome prior to the event itself. To avoid the intense daytime heat, many riders leave their quarters in the early hours of the morning to perform the mentally and physically exhausting work-outs in the relative cool of the tree-shaded gardens. Horse-boxes ferry their fares backwards and forwards between the Villa Glori Stables and the training area in an elaborate timetable

'Trish Galvin, the accomplished American dressage rider, hears trainer Jean Paillard's comments on her work with Rathpatrick. (Miss Galvin returned to her hotel bedroom after each training session to be nursed for 'flu.) M. Paillard trains all of those Galvin horses which are quartered in Paris

1956 Gold Medal winner Henri St Cyr (Sweden), takes his newcomer L'Etoile through a passage movement

Mr Fred Broome works Sunsalve in the Gardens. David Broome and Mr Oliver Anderson's extraordinary chestnut horse carry off a Bronze Medal for Britain in the Individual Showjumping event. At the end of the week, their afternoon round in the Prix des Nations goes down as a moral triumph. An award of four faults for an infringement at the water-jump (later disproved by film cameras) robs them of the only clear round of the whole enormous competition

Conversano Caprice in the Villa Glori Stables

Twenty-one-year-old David takes Sunsalve over a training jump

Pat Smythe has the great distinction of being the only woman rider to appear in the Stadio Olimpico—and what a cool, precise appearance it is! Trusty Flanagan has carried Pat at two Olympic Games, and their picture appeared in colour on the cover of a Rome newspaper

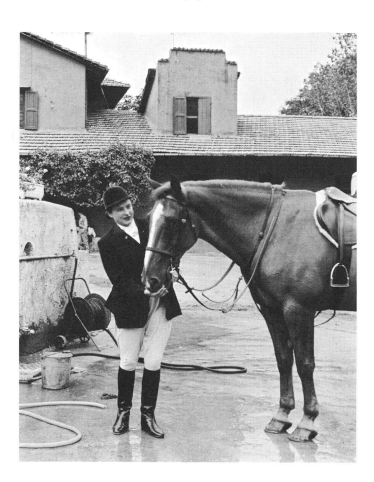

**15,000
MILES
TO THE
GAMES . . .**

New Zealander Adrian White, assisted by John Howard, took Mrs H. D. Macdonald's Telebrae to the Games as an individual entry. Undaunted by the fact of only having one horse, their efforts were matched by Telebrae's fitness and fortitude. The pictures on this page show the journey through Tuscany after leaving Rome

After a sea voyage from New Zealand to England, during which time an obliging Captain allowed the phlegmatic Telebrae to be exercised around the decks, training was continued in England prior to departure for the Continent. The New Zealanders' efficient performances created interest wherever they went, and even while bivouacked in the byres of lonely farmsteads, Telebrae's healthy physique was the cynosure of many shrewd eyes. Few could comprehend where the horse had indeed travelled from

LEFT Adrian White and Telebrae are one of the first combinations to enter the Piazza di Siena; the successful conclusion to a great adventure. Their afternoon round of twelve faults proves to be one of the best performances in the second half

27

British riders at the Villa Glori Stables: Bertie Hill, David Barker and Norman Arthur

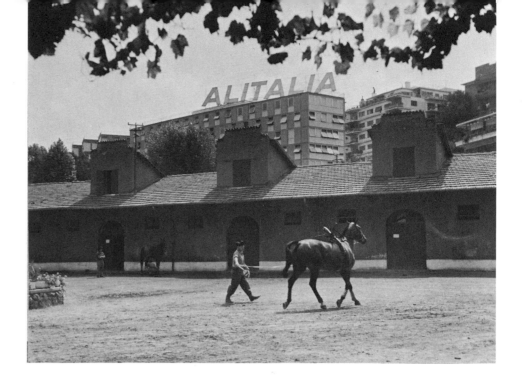

AUSTRALIAN ENDEAVOUR

In the dusty, disordered plateau of Pratoni del Vivaro, high in the hills beyond Rome, facilities lacked the glamour that was imparted by the city itself. For all that, the performances were courageous in the extreme. After two days of dressage tests under trying conditions with a laissez-faire attitude prevailing where organization was concerned, the riders vacated the dressage area—to the resident hens' relief—and tackled the awesome cross country course. By great good fortune a slight breeze and thin cloud tempered conditions on the Cross Country day and the heavy rain experienced earlier in the week had in some way mitigated the paralysing amount of dust, as well as taking the worst sting from the ground. It is impossible to recount all the changes of fortune in a day that was as mentally fatiguing for onlookers as it was physically exhausting for competitors, but leading memories must be of the Australians performing quite magnificently. Lawrence Morgan and Salad Days went a great pace, cutting large slices from the jumping course by making stockman-like short cuts through the scrub, suddenly appearing from nowhere to the amazement of officials and disconcerted spectators, who were often caught where they should not have been. It was rumoured that Salad Days' time was a whole minute within the time required for maximum bonus points.

Of the remaining Australians, Neil Lavis with Mirrabooka and Brian Crago with Sabre were both clear, and it was only Bill Roycroft and the gallant little Our Solo that had any trouble. By the concrete pipes fence they had the misfortune to stumble in a rabbit hole. Badly shaken, Bill Roycroft remounted and completed the course, before being taken to hospital with a cracked collarbone and strained neck ligaments. The Australians were still in a wonderful position, with Lawrence Morgan's 144 bonus points over the Cross Country giving him an overall plus score of 37·94, Brian Crago had a plus score of 5·09 in second place, and Neil Lavis was third with −16·50.

Captain Harry Freeman Jackson and St Finbarr went superbly well for the excellent Irish team, and for Britain, it was Michael Bullen and Col. Williams' grey mare Cottage Romance who really triumphed over the course. At the end of the Cross Country day the points were:

AUSTRALIA : +26·53 SWITZERLAND : −252·22 IRELAND : −407·51

FRANCE : −430·51 GREAT BRITAIN : −467·80

The rest of the story was none too happy. Neither of the first two riders from the following countries managed to get round the course, meaning that the United States of America, Rumania, Bulgaria, Russia, Canada, Sweden, Spain and Argentina were all eliminated. Portugal, Germany and Poland fell by the wayside during the afternoon, to complete a strong indictment of the severe course—or perhaps more important, the gruelling Roads and Tracks phase that preceded it. Back in the green and ordered surroundings of the Piazza di Siena the next day, there took place the culmination of the great efforts at Pratoni del Vivaro. Undoubtedly the biggest tragedy from the Australian point of view was the fact that Brian Crago's Sabre had gone unsound, necessitating withdrawal and thus robbing his rider of a certain medal. To maintain the team position, Bill Roycroft was required to remove himself from hospital—in the face of dire threats by the staff, who finally realized that even if they hid their patient's clothes he would have walked to the arena naked. Salad Days and Mirrabooka both went faultlessly over the showjumping course, but it was Bill Roycroft, strapped and full of injections, who won the wildest cheers of the day with as immaculate a clear round as one could ever wish to see. His heroic effort clinched his country's richly deserved Gold Medal. Lawrence Morgan had the Individual Gold Medal well and truly in his pocket, while Neil Lavis had moved up over the hapless Brian Crago. How near the Australians came to first, second *and* third! The green and gold quarter cloths of the Australian horses were prized possessions up in the remote and almost forgotten Pratoni stables that evening. What gallant horses those rugs graced.

Many strange anecdotes surround the Rome Olympics, but one of the less well-known ones and perhaps, more humourous ones, concerns Australia's Brian Crago, the luckless rider who was forced eventually to withdraw his mount when in sight of a silver medal. During the Roads and Tracks phase of the Three-Day Event, the Australians' eye for country and their shrewd teamwork discovered many labour-saving short cuts through the uncleared scrub of the Pratoni estate. At one stage, Brian Crago—and a coolly fresh Sabre—emerged onto a recognized track from one such deviation, in time to notice the figure of another horse and rider in the distance behind. With more than enough time in hand, Crago ambled along in a relaxed manner. The following rider gradually closed the gap—it was in fact France's Jean Le Roy, *preceding* rider in the lists. Suddenly, the Frenchman became aware of Crago's number: "Forty-*five*—and going so slowly!" But he—Le Roy, was number forty-*four*. What had happened? "Mon Dieu! I *must* be late!" With a flurry of activity, Le Roy and Garden passed the bemused Crago in a cloud of dust, and it was only when Crago spotted the number of the fast disappearing Frenchman that the reason for such anguished behaviour became clear. There were some puzzled post-mortems in the French camp that evening, and Le Roy's explanation is still regarded with some suspicion by his team mates.

A PERSONAL PLEA
FOR LESS SEVERE
OLYMPIC COURSES

Rome
1960

Edward Harty and Harlequin, members of the splendid Irish team which loses a certain medal through a tragic technical disqualification on the final day

Michael Bullen and Col. Williams' grey mare Cottage Romance—fourth in the Individual honours at Rome

*For the showjumpers, a devilish treble causes untold strife during the Individual
event at the Piazza di Siena. Studying the problem with grave faces are
members of Great Britain's team: Dawn Wofford, Pat Smythe, David Broome,
trainer Jack Talbot-Ponsonby and Chef d'Equipe Harry Llewellyn*

Part of the Irish contingent walks the sobering course. Left to right: Lt. Daly, Lt. O'Donohoe, Col. Neylon (Chef d'Equipe) and reserve rider Capt. Molony

Not one of the Borghese statues, but a non-Roman spectator embellishing a convenient fountain

Swiss rider Anton Bühler and Gay Spark clear the top obstacle . . .

. . . an exhausted horse in Samuel Johnson clears the next stage . . .

. . . and a bloodstained Major Pierre Durand and Gulliano drop into the road; a sequence of obstacles towards the end of the Cross Country course which is responsible for many eliminations

Hans Schwarzenbach (Switzerland) and Burn Trout manage well . . .

. . . so does the ultimate Gold Medallist Lawrence Morgan and Salad Days. LEFT *The Australian team captain chooses his place and (*BELOW*) in the afternoon clears the same spot precisely, having given himself a vital extra stride by swinging diagonally across the road before leaping out*

Greetings on the steeplechase course: Mrs Bertie Hill, Lt.-Col. Harry Llewellyn and Major Derek Allhusen

Colonel Mike Ansell and Dorian Williams—with shirt trouble

ABOVE *Lt.-Col. Frank Weldon, the British Three-Day Event team captain, sets a scorching pace at the beginning of their round, but the story is sadly different later*

LEFT *Bertie Hill's first fall on Wild Venture comes at Fence 2. The firm grip certainly doesn't save the situation, but loose earth on the take-off side has already brought their leap to nought, though surprisingly well clear of the landing edge as it transpires*

CROSS-COUNTRY
COURSE AT
PRATONI DEL VIVARO

LITTLE MODEL'S TRIP TO ROME

With a tendency to claustrophobia in particularly confined spaces, Little Model was one of the British horses that did not travel by air. The road journey from England was frequently broken so that Mrs Williams might ride her dressage horse each day as the entourage pressed steadily southwards. While the rest of the party made tea Mrs Williams rode ahead along the quieter country roads of France, before being overtaken by the horse-box. The sight of *la dame anglaise* making sprightly and eye-catching progress through villages of boggle-eyed inhabitants was one of the happier memories of the Olympic trip. The method proved to be a surprisingly successful way of getting a fit and happy horse from A to Z.

Ready for the daily stint

The Mont Genevre snowline

The commencement of it all

Dawn at Dunkirk

THE TRIP
CONTINUES

Breakfast time in a Briançon hotel yard

 *hidden*

The road to Soissons

LEFT *At Briançon in the French Alps, with a morning stretch from Mo' as the dawn sky lightens above the monastery*

A customs delay at the Italian frontier put to good purpose . . .

. . . with some engaging light relief . . .

. . . and some mountainside exercises

The morning walk to the Piazza di Siena, with the trip's culmination in sight . . .
. . . and emergence after a particularly pleasing and well-received display in the
Gran Premio di Dressage

Henri Chammartin (Switzerland) and Wolfdietrich give the poetically smooth dressage display that is expected of them. The elegant figure in the bottom left corner is Hugh Wiley

Bill Steinkraus and Riviera Wonder

The American captain with Ksar d'Esprit

The United States Equestrian team for the 1960 Olympics: Left to right, William Steinkraus, George Morris, Frank Chapot and Hugh Wiley

The Prince of Wales Cup, which the American 1960 Olympic team won at London's Royal International Horse Show for three years in succession, is a tangible symbol of the uniformly high standard these riders maintained during their three years of strenuous campaigning throughout Europe prior to the Olympic Games. Bill Steinkraus, the gifted team captain, has been at the forefront of international competition on a variety of famous mounts, and he has represented his country at three Olympic Games. The horse which comes closest to Bill Steinkraus' own ideals is Riviera Wonder, owned by Mr and Mrs Bernie Mann. This versatile and stylish grey, who has the great asset of complete adaptability to varying types of competition, is seen (TOP LEFT) jumping with the handy elasticity of a cat—ready to turn in the final of a speed competition. Bill's Olympic mount Ksar d'Esprit is one of the world's great Puissance horses. A formidable grey, he was bred in Maryland by Hugh Wiley, sold to Canada for a period, and eventually bought back for the American team by Miss Eleanora Sears, in whose ownership he remains. He is by the French-bred sire Ksar, out of Coq d'Esprit.

Exceptional poise and balance were two of the attributes of the American 1960 Olympic team, which made an immediate impression on its first European tour in 1958. The youngest rider was George Morris, who won the Individual Trophy at Dublin that year. George has now forsaken his riding career for an equally promising one on the stage, but not before coming within a point of David Broome's Bronze Medal score at Rome. In the year that George Morris won in Dublin, Hugh Wiley opened his account at London's White City Stadium, where he won the King George V Gold Cup with the grey Master William. The following year, the inimitable Nautical gave Hugh a second great win in this event. Bill Steinkraus is the only other American rider to have won this most coveted trophy for the world's male riders. In 1956 he finished with the only two clear rounds on Night Owl and First Boy, nominating the latter as the winner.

Hugh Wiley (U.S.A.) on Master William

LEFT *George Morris (U.S.A.) on Mrs John Galvin's Night Owl*

Trail Guide—the horse with the best score of the American team at two Olympic Games. Seen above with Hugh Wiley, who rode him in the 1956 Olympics, the then aged chestnut has—in this picture—caused his rider a somewhat untypical loss of stirrup position, but safely over for all that. BELOW Hugh Wiley with his famed and popular partner Nautical, now in retirement

OPPOSITE With her Lippizaner dressage horse Conversano Caprice, Mrs Robert Hall talks to Colonel Francke of Switzerland during a dawn training session in the Borghese Gardens, Rome

In the 1960 Olympics, Trail Guide was partnered by Frank Chapot, seen (BELOW) in impeccable position on Tally Ho. Trail Guide was a horse whose magnificent condition totally belied his advanced years; Frank Chapot was mounted on the horse when it died suddenly during a fall at Madison Square Gardens in 1961. For a rider who dabbles with steeplechase riding, Frank can still provide a lesson in secure and deep seat position—a heritage of Bertalan de Nemethy's matchless training.

Frank Chapot on Miss 'Trish Galvin's Tally Ho

Hugh Wiley on San Pedro, London 1962

Hugh Wiley landing on Trail Guide in 1959. Another King George V Cup winner, David Broome, is seen (RIGHT) at a similar moment with Sunsalve

Sue Cohen (now Sue Welch) and Clare Castle were members of the British team that competed at the 1961 Rome International Show. Sue had won the Ladies' European Championship at Copenhagen in 1960, and the same year she also won the Queen Elizabeth II Cup in London. In 1961 the combination won the South of England Ladies' Championship at Brighton for the second time

Pat Smythe and Scorchin' (G.B.)

The final of a speed competition at the White City, London. Three of the riders are already sizing up the next jump; one is more concerned with clearing the obstacle in hand—which he did

Bay Lane and Trueman II (G.B.)

P. Mayorga and Stromboli (Argentina)

Frank Chapot and Trail Guide (U.S.A.)

BADMINTON 1961

1961, and nearly 'the Badminton that wasn't' for Lawrence Morgan. Only a week before the event, Salad Days was still performing with his owner under National Hunt Rules. After the decision to declare for the Badminton event, two losses of memory in the Dressage phase brought the pair close to an untimely elimination. Their troubles were not over. On the second day, a traffic block held up horse and rider, causing them to arrive at the starting post both late and hot, and only a delay to the preceding competitor saved the situation. During the Cross Country phase, Morgan treated a depression in the approach to a double rails with undue caution, thereby losing impulsion and coming close to disaster at the obstacle itself. But it was disaster avoided and the pair got through unpenalized, though an error in the official tabulation of marks sent the Australian rider to bed that night believing that he was trailing the Irishman Captain Harry Freeman Jackson. In fact, their positions were reversed, and clear rounds by both protagonists in the final day's showjumping meant that Lawrence Morgan had maintained his slender lead for the coveted title.

Lawrence Morgan and Salad Days (Australia)

Captain Harry Freeman Jackson and St Finbarr (Ireland)

Miss Lana du Pont and Mr Wister (U.S.A.) give a most workmanlike display over the three days at Badminton, 1961, for a final placing of tenth in the main event

M. A. Le Goupil (France) on Jacasse Bat Fence 25, The Drop

Almost a moment of undoing for Lawrence Morgan at Fence 26 but he sits tight and Salad Days scrapes painfully over and continues on his way untroubled and unpenalized. They retain their slender lead over St Finbarr with a very necessary clear round on the third day

Lt. the Hon. Patrick Conolly-Carew with the chestnut mare Ballyhoo—one of the most consistent combinations in British horse trials. Ballyhoo went for eighteen months without having a fence down

BRITISH ARMY
HORSE TRIALS

TIDWORTH 1961

Another pair to make their presence known in the trials world—
Sergeant Jones of the King's Troup, R.H.A., on Sherpa

LEFT *The Gladiator, ridden by Susan Fleet, one of the younger*
British riders that have represented their country abroad

WINDSOR SHOW
1961

Mrs Judy Crago on Thou Swell

Winner of a trade turn-out class

LEFT *Musical ride of the Household Cavalry*

RIGHT *Alan Oliver on Red Admiral*

63

AACHEN 1961

David Broome—European Men's Showjumping Champion for 1961—on Mr Oliver Anderson's Sunsalve

After twice coming second to Piero d'Inzeo in the first two events which contribute towards the Championship, the twenty-one-year-old British rider manages to beat Graziano Mancinelli in the third and final event, thus clinching sufficient points to win the Championship—the first occasion it has been won by a Britisher. Mancinelli later won the title for himself in 1963.

Unlike Rome 1960, where Sunsalve's majestic progress was relatively calm and orderly, the tension at Aachen is more obviously manifest in Sunsalve's wide eyes and steam-train acceleration. Coming into the difficult treble at the end of the final Championship event, the pair cause British supporters to clutch each other in suspense, but the sheer muscle power of the chestnut's hindquarters sees them through unscathed; the title is theirs.

With the sun setting, the awards are made, and David lets Sunsalve have his head for a moment as they begin to leave the arena. Almost immediately the brakes have to be applied again as the rider calls "Whoa!" and eyes the barrier at the ring entrance. It goes up in time, and they sweep out in truly conquering fashion.

The tension is over and the spoils of victory make their appearance. Graziano Mancinelli is thoughtful. Had he been able to beat Sunsalve in the final event, his compatriot Piero d'Inzeo might have got the title. However, the British anthem is played for what appears to be a most popular victory

Later, in his Aachen hotel, David Broome ponders his fortune, manifest in the beautiful trophy which graces the team table—no doubt to the slight chagrin of some other diners!

Phlegmatic Scorchin', in the hands of his owner, begins to learn that corner cutting can be brought to a fine art—with the result that they are no longer a force to overlook when the clock is on

68

Fritz Thiedemann and Godewind were given a clear round in this event. Charity begins at home, but it was later extended to David Broome in a somewhat suspect situation at the same jump. Until some more cast-iron method of judging is devised, there will always be controversies at water-jumps

A successful show for Anna Clement and Nico (Germany), with three speed-event wins to their credit. Nico's ability to twist and turn over a course stood them in good stead in the final of the 1959 Queen Elizabeth II Cup, which they won

An essential prelude to jumpinge walking the course. Capt. d: Llano, David Broome and Mary Barnes

Modern electronics heighten the presentation for television viewers with amplified sound effects. Josef Neckerman Jnr takes Raubautz on to the Table

71

Pat Smythe and Scorchin', third in the Puissance

Two horses without a martingale; one with. Now little to choose between them in the way of head carriage . . .

Piero d'Inzeo (Italy) and Sunbeam

. . . but one pair of hands working slightly differently
from those of the other two riders.

—*Graziano Mancinelli on Frau Piaggio's Gentleman*

FENCES

Part of the charm of Aachen lies in the abundance and variety of fences encountered there. They are built at strategic points in the large arena and often make use of water as a natural element. Alwin Schockemöhle and Freiherr, winners of the German Grand Prix at Aachen in 1962, negotiate the 'out' section of the road crossing (RIGHT). Horses find the jumps intriguing and invariably tackle them with relish; on the big galloping course there is room for them to stretch out in a long stride between fences.

The reconstruction of fences in the event of a knock-down (BELOW) is always as painstaking as the original labour. The obstacle must be precisely the same for each competitor.

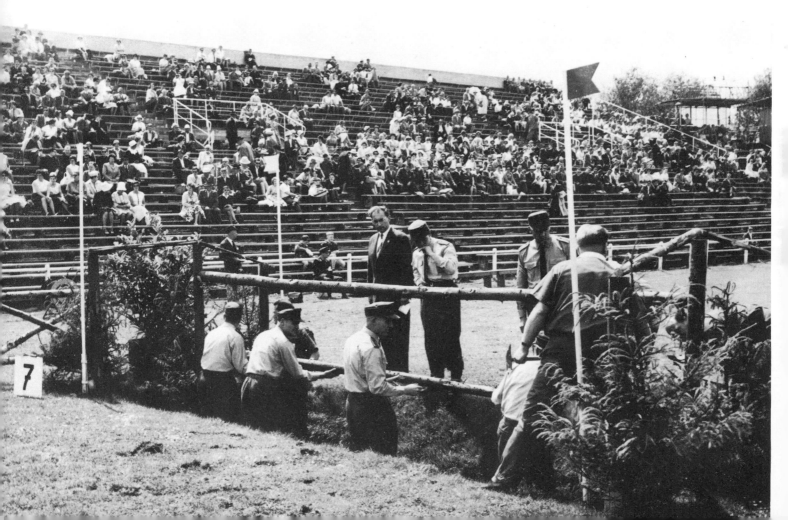

The Belgian rider J. P. Seynaeve on Dorn, takes the final fence in a speed event against the clock

Mary Barnes and Sudden (G.B.) launch themselves off the Aachen Table. This pair won the Take-Your-Own-Line Competition in 1961, ahead of B. Lilov of Russia and S. Hobolt-Jensen of Denmark

RIGHT *Ann Townsend and Frenchman's Creek, another British pair, making a quartet in the Aachen Pond—a refreshing interlude on hot days, but one which adds insult to injury on the really damp days one occasionally experiences at Aachen*

Another meticulously constructed fence, with rustic components—
this time tackled with the recognizable efficiency of the great
Fritz Thiedemann and Meteor

RIGHT *The fluent Brazilian rider Nelson Pessoa makes a
confident flight off the Aachen Table with Espartaco*

Bay Lane and Trueman II
(G.B.) treat the same obstacle
with a little more caution

An accepted part of the Aachen scene are the classes for carriage horses; events which draw large entries from the host nation, and which also prove popular with competitors from Hungary and Yugoslavia. Milling in the big arena together, they match the fountain in gaiety and sparkle

BELOW *The postilion of a Hungarian entry*

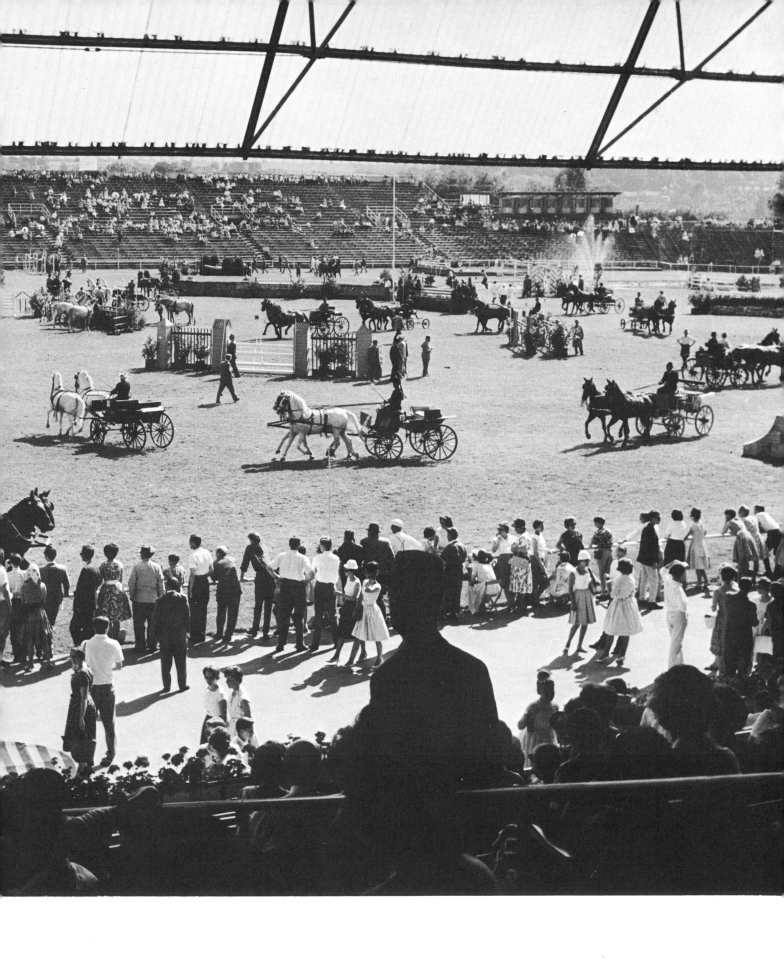

A vehicle with a more mundane task ahead of it goes about its business

RIGHT *Showing presence and finesse, a leading pair from a Yugoslav carriage team: Siglavy Batosta and Siglavy Serena*

Carlos Figueroa of Spain, on his Anglo-Arab jumper Lorrain

RIGHT *Nelson Pessoa displays his usual adroitness—here with Espartaco*

84

In the first F.E.I. competition at the 1961 Aachen Show, Great Britain's George Hobbs and Royal Lord tied for first place with the Italian combination of Piero d'Inzeo and Sunbeam. In third place was Pat Smythe and Flanagan—though she is on Scorchin' for the presentation

One of the greatest names in international show-jumping, Fritz Thiedemann, concluded his career at the 1961 Aachen Show. It was fitting that his last appearance in the ring as an active competitor should be as a member of the German team in the Nations' event. Godewind crowned his own career as a partner for Fritz with no jumping faults in either of the two rounds—a strong contribution to their country's win.

LEFT *The popular rider immediately after riding for his country for the last time*

Fritz Thiedemann and Godewind

Nelson Pessoa and Espartaco launch themselves over a rustic fence in their customary smooth parabola. The stylish Brazilian's showing on the European circuit has been conspicuously successful

LEFT Hans Günter Winkler and Feuerdorn cope impeccably with the Aachen Table. With hindlegs neatly together for maximum impulsion, this statuesque pose is part of a faultless approach to the obstacle—one which the great German rider makes appear deceptively easy

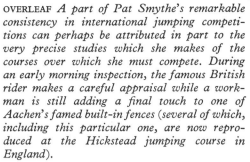

OVERLEAF *A part of Pat Smythe's remarkable consistency in international jumping competitions can perhaps be attributed in part to the very precise studies which she makes of the courses over which she must compete. During an early morning inspection, the famous British rider makes a careful appraisal while a workman is still adding a final touch to one of Aachen's famed built-in fences (several of which, including this particular one, are now reproduced at the Hickstead jumping course in England).*

Later on the same day, Pat gives another fence more reflective scrutiny while walking the course with fellow riders.

Aachen 1961, and the farewell appearance of two national favourites. Fritz Thiedemann and Meteor, deserved heroes of the show ring, take every precaution to ensure that the final round of their career together is a clear one. Fritz's cautionary glance at the rail is unnecessary—the double Gold Medal pair are home without fault to set the seal on a partnership as legendary as that of Harry Llewellyn and Foxhunter, or Winkler and Halla. In a moving presentation, Meteor was given a year's supply of oats to take with him into retirement.

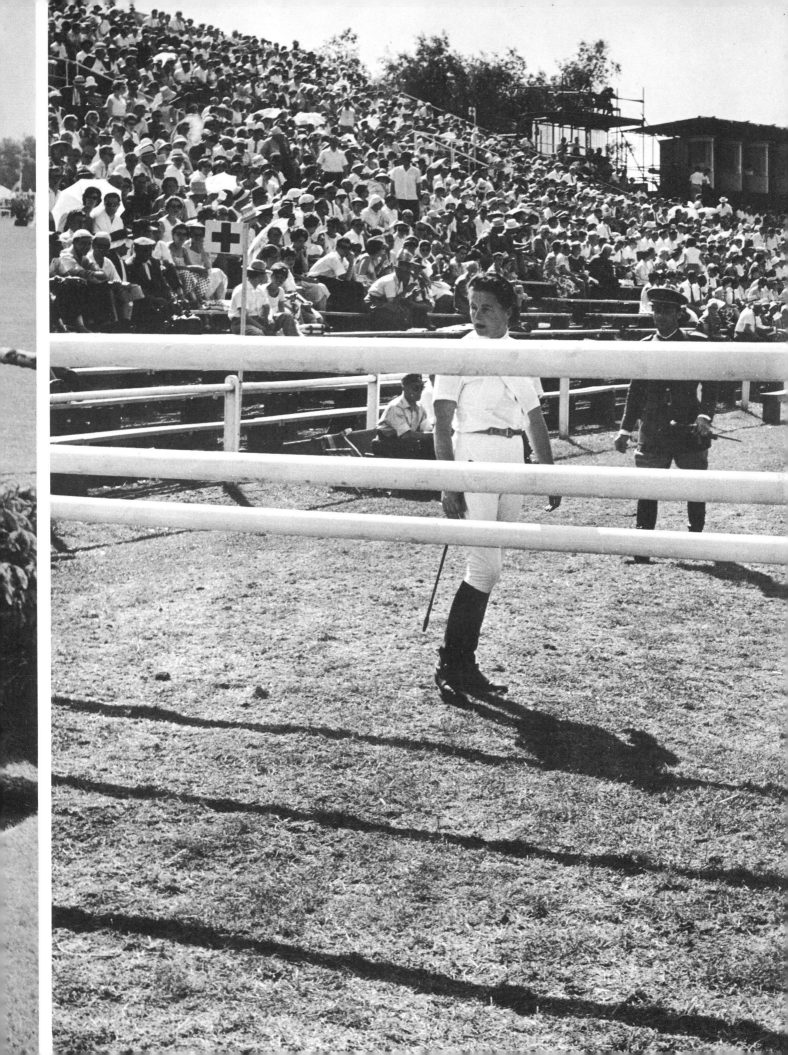

*Pat Smythe continues serenely on her winning way,
this time annexing the Prix des Dames with Flanagan*

First down to breakfast with a busy day ahead—Britain's Chef d'Equipe, Colonel "Nat" Kindersley

LEFT A rider's neccessary duty before an event—studying the starting list

97

The sand may be hot but the spectators are few—a good opportunity for a practice work-out. German Bronze Medallist Josef Neckermann and Asbach iron out a performance which later earned the judges' approval to the extent of winning the European Dressage Championship

Entente cordiale between Sergei Filatov, Russia's Gold Medallist, and Liselott Linsenhoff, German Bronze Medallist in 1956. Learning a test presents translation problems

Russian rider Vtorov, working Korbei in one of the practice dressage arenas

Watching intently—Col. and Mrs V. D. S. Williams

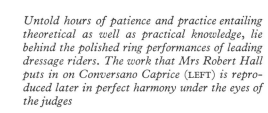

Untold hours of patience and practice entailing theoretical as well as practical knowledge, lie behind the polished ring performances of leading dressage riders. The work that Mrs Robert Hall puts in on Conversano Caprice (LEFT) is reproduced later in perfect harmony under the eyes of the judges

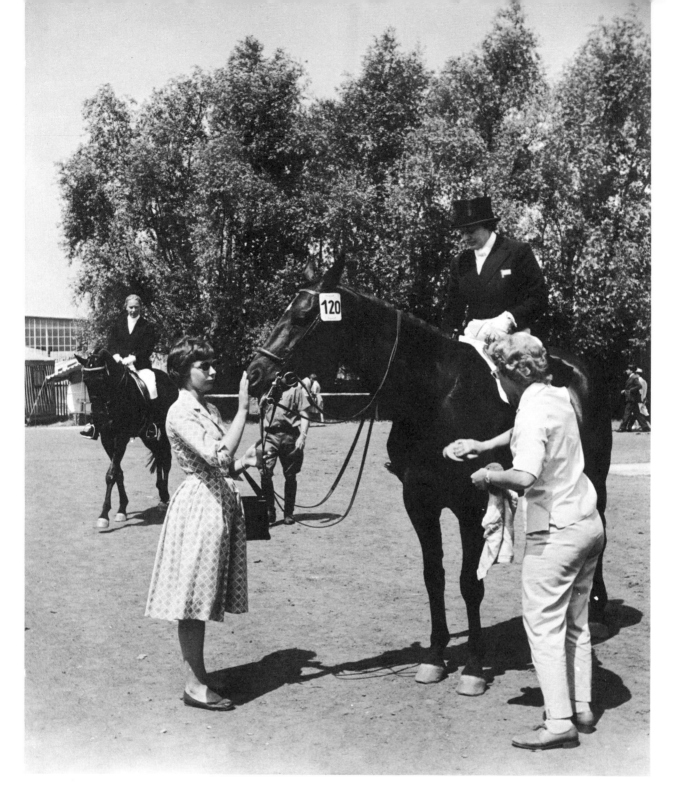

For Frau Springer there is a welcome return to the shade after
their test, but for Mrs Joan Gold and Gay Gordon there is the
last minute 'spit-and-polish' before displaying their skill

Other riders take the chance to continue the practical development

Absent in the extended trot

at the canter

Sergei Filatov, ebullient Russian master of the iron hand in the velvet glove. A friendly man who cuts the mystique of *haute ecole* riding with his willingness to give one an intricate practical demonstration of a point under discussion, Filatov also knows how to draw a gallery's attention—and he does it supremely well. There are few people who can produce the 'goods' for the customers the way he can. Much hard work goes into the eye-catching displays the Russian gives on the black entire, Absent. The horse comes from jumping stock, and in lighter moments is allowed to *passage* up to a 4-foot rail and hop over it with disdainful ease; yet another skill guaranteed to impress anyone lucky enough to see it.

Even Mrs Williams, a particularly experienced huntswoman, is caught a fraction unawares by Mo's joie de vivre in this test jump. The Connemara strain is showing its paces!

LITTLE MODEL

the extended trot

Prince Bernhard of the Netherlands talking with Col. and Mrs Williams

Mrs V. D. S. Williams' meritorious third to Josef Neckermann and Sergei Filatov is a highlight of the European Grand Prix Dressage Championship competition. It is the first time a British rider has achieved a place in such a competition, and it helps to reflect credit on the strides that British dressage riding has taken in a comparatively short time.

ECONOMY OF ACTION

Peter Robeson's meticulous attention to jumping style in a horse produces classic results in the art of basculing, but this noteworthy fluidity and lack of extravagance does not make for a spectacular photograph. The action must speak for itself in the results achieved.

Peter Robeson made a most welcome return to the winning lists in international competitions with Firecrest, an Irish-bred horse that jumped well in Scotland before being taken in hand by his present owner, who successfully remodelled the horse's whole style of jumping. They triumphed in the Imperial Cup at the 1961 Royal International, and were also the chief architects of Britain's win in the Nations Cup at Rotterdam that year. In the Championship at Rome in 1962, the combination was one-tenth of a second behind The Rock's winning time.

Not a victory rostrum this time, but it might well be. Italy's Gold
Medallist and winner of the World Championship title at Venice
in 1960, Raimondo d'Inzeo, surveys the scene at London the
following summer

Always a source of discomfort to opponents, Graziano Mancinelli won the Country Life and Riding Cup, the Daily Mail Cup, and was second in the John Player Trophy—all with the grey mare Rockette who helped Mancinelli win the Men's European Championship for 1963

The great Merano, who made further appearances at the White City in 1961 and 1962. Slipping around speed courses with a facility that belied his somewhat 'veteran' status, lop-eared Merano brought to mind his great days as an Olympic horse and No. 1 mount for the World Champion. On this particular reunion with English audiences in 1961, Merano scored in the Maidens and Knaves Stakes and was a member of the winning Italian team in the Prince of Wales Cup.

The World Champion views a humorist's touch with an appraising eye, before rising to the situation with a floral tribute . . .

RAIMONDO AND
THE WATER SPRITE

. . . later, Raimondo d'Inzeo and Merano take a more serious approach to the water-jump

Renate Freitag of Germany with Winzer, a specialist over big jumps

Alwin Schockemöhle has a calmly businesslike approach to show-jumping that keeps him prominent in strong international competition. RIGHT *On his Olympic mount Ferdl, at London, 1961*

Raimondo d'Inzeo's slightly-built chestnut horse Posillipo became a world name in show-jumping almost overnight with spectacular performances over the testing courses at the 1960 Olympics. The genius may be in the saddle, but here it finds a very willing counterpart

The most sensational win at the 1961 Royal International was undoubtedly that of Pat Smythe and Scorchin' in the newly inaugurated £1000 John Player Trophy Championship. Five finalists were left with two clear rounds apiece. In a particularly formidable jump-off against the clock, a capacity crowd came to its feet with a mighty roar as showjumping's First Lady clipped a fifth of a second off a remarkable time set by Graziano Mancinelli. Going even faster in a desperate attempt to meet the challenge, Raimondo d'Inzeo had the last fence down, leaving the prize in British hands. Her Majesty the Queen presented the trophy for a truly memorable performance.

Third in the 1961 John Player Trophy was the indomitable Oorskiet, the 14.3½ h.h. miracle, ridden as always, by his owner, Lady Sarah FitzAlan Howard. This courageous effort was but part of a week that had already seen the pair triumph in the coveted Queen Elizabeth II Cup for Lady Riders, a result that merely confirmed their strong international rating

WALKING THE COURSE

is an art in itself. The thought applied at this stage is reflected in the subsequent performances . . .

Alan Oliver keeps an eye on Ted Williams' measured tread and later that of Peter Robeson

. . . and there is always the job of putting them up in the first place

Kathy Kusner (U.S.A.) jots it down on paper for reference at a later date

Two champions: David Barker (G.B.) with Raimondo d'Inzeo (Italy)

Mary Mairs and Tomboy (U.S.A.)

LEFT *Sarah FitzAlan Howard,
David Broome (visiting only, on
this occasion) and Pierre Durand*

Cloyne

An Irishman with a purpose, Billy Ringrose has built himself into the international scene with solid achievements. Perhaps most memorable to date were his performances at the 1961 Rome International Horse Show, where he broke the d'Inzeo brothers' stranglehold on the winner's rostrum. After a first and second with Cloyne and Ceannanus Mor in the Premio Piazza di Siena, Ringrose scored a sparkling win with Loch an Easpaig in the major event, the Gran Premio di Roma, adding for good measure second place with Cloyne. With the latter, Ringrose collected a win in the Premio Aventino almost as an afterthought. This form continued to be in evidence during a North American tour late in 1961.

Dublin retains its grip on the imagination, and successive visits only add to a visitor's infatuation. The pearls of wisdom and blarney heard around the perimeters of the hunters' rings leave one happy for weeks. At no other sales rings in the world is money extracted so agreeably.

DUBLIN 1961

Judged instead of judging this time: 'Tricia Hanson retains her usual elegance

OPPOSITE *Fritz Thiedemann's young
protégé Kurt Jarasinski won the
Lonsdale Puissance Championship with
Rafaella, London 1962*

FAMILIAR
NAMES
AT
DUBLIN

Dressing from the right: Judge Wylie, pillar of the Ball's Bridge Establishment

The Hon. Diana Conolly-Carew demonstrates her acquaintance with Irish banks—this time on Barrymore

BELOW *Year after year the hunter rings at Ball's Bridge Showgrounds come up with a seemingly inexhaustible supply of quality stock.* RIGHT *Mrs David Price with her 1961 Champion Ladies' Hunter, The Baronet.* BELOW RIGHT *In 1961 the top honour in the Dublin hunter classes went to an exceedingly popular combination of Lady Helena Hilton-Green and Last of the Banogues. A proven performer across country, the six-year-old hunter looked all the part leaving the ring after the traditional parade*

Lady Helena Hilton-Green

Mr Robert Hanson's Canadian purchase O'Malley, jumping in
Dublin under the guidance of Harvey Smith. The British pair
had won the 1962 John Player Trophy in London a week
previously and the following year saw the Rome Grand Prix
among their trophies

LEFT *One of Spain's most fluent military combinations,
that of Capt. Alfonso Queipo de Llano and Eolo 4*

Mme Arline Givaudan (Brazil) on the
former Argentine Olympic horse, Huipil

After a fairly torrid time in London in 1961, the German team struck form with a vengeance in Dublin. They notched an unassailable lead in the team event, the Aga Khan Trophy. Parading after their victory (ABOVE) the team consists of: Hans Günter Winkler on Romanus, Herman Schridde on Fugosa, Alwin Schockemöhle on Ferdl and Thomas Bagusat on Bajazzo III

A remarkably similar scene presented itself when the Italian team won the trophy exactly a year later. This time it is Piero d'Inzeo on The Rock, Doctor Ugo d'Amelio on Fancy Socks, Raimondo d'Inzeo on Posillipo and Graziano Mancinelli on Rockette (winner of the Boylan Memorial Trophy for 1962)

Winner of the 1961 Dublin Puissance after a record battle in such an event at Dublin, the German ace Winkler on Romanus clearing the Wall—here at 6 feet 8 inches

the Wall at 6 feet

MASTERFUL
CONSISTENCY

Major Piero d'Inzeo's ring performances indicate untold patience in
training behind the scenes. His
horses are among the few present-
day jumpers that perform without
any type of martingale (Scorchin'
and Firecrest are others that come
to mind), although onlookers, noting
in the Italian's horses a recent tendency towards high head carriage
might feel this bit of equipment an
advantage. Whatever they do with
their heads, there is no denying
that great troupers like The Rock
continue to trounce the world's
best.

Here, in successive jump-offs in
a Puissance at Dublin, Piero and
The Rock display the precision that
has earned them the distinction of

the Wall at 6 feet 4 inches

being the first *combination* to
annex the King George V Gold
Cup in two successive years. Having
already won the trophy in 1957
with Uruguay, Piero's rousing 1962
win against his brother Raimondo
earned him a place in the special
niche occupied by Jack Talbot-
Ponsonby and Harry Llewellyn as
the only riders to have claimed the
trophy on three separate occasions.
A delightful and amusing character
off duty, Piero was virtually invinc-
ible in the Grand Prix events of
Europe during 1962. Italian F.E.I.
bureaucracy was responsible for
severing this famous partnership
early in 1963.

the Wall at 6 feet 8 inches

Formerly owned by Hugh Wiley, Hollandia first achieved prominence as the mount of Bill Steinkraus in the 1952 Olympic Games. Bought later by fellow American Warren Wofford (now domiciled in England), the gallant Hollandia later carried Warren's British wife Dawn in the Individual event at the 1960 Olympics. ABOVE *Warren Wofford and Hollandia, still going strong in the finals of the Puissance at Dublin in 1961*

In 1961, to the rapturous delight of onlookers, pint-sized Dundrum swept all before him in three international events (and two national ones), finally winning the Ball's Bridge Trophy for his rider Tommy Wade, who might well pick his legs up out of harm's way—Dundrum is only fractionally bigger than a pony! At Wembley in 1959, this stag-like little bay horse cleared a wall at seven feet, and at Wembley in 1961 the pair won the Victor Ludorum event on the final evening of the show. After a brilliant Spring Show in Dublin, 1962 saw them again in England, this time winning the £500 Vaux Gold Tankard, and coming second to Flanagan in the British Jumping Derby. Back in Dublin, they eclipsed Piero d'Inzeo and The Rock in the Top Score Competition. A horse with a heart as big as himself.

Tommy Wade and Mr James Wade's Dundrum

In 1961, Nelson Pessoa maintained the promise he had shown on earlier excursions, hitting the front rank and staying there. The grey Gran Geste was the cynosure of all eyes with his expertise over Puissance courses. The Brazilian resisted offers for purchase and continued to delight connoisseurs of good riding with poise and precision over a variety of competitions. Gran Geste won the Lonsdale Puissance in London in July, 1961. Seen here at Dublin the following month, where they were second to Dundrum in the Boylan Memorial Trophy. Pessoa and Gran Geste just beat Pat Smythe and Telebrae in the final of the Grand Prix at St Gall, Switzerland, later that year. Also winners of the Grand Prix d'Europe at Aachen in 1962 beating Bill Steinkraus and Sinjon.

Nelson Pessoa and Gran Geste

David Broome on Mr Oliver Anderson's Sunsalve

Pat Smythe on Mr Robert Hanson's Flanagan

A RECORD TREBLE

1961 was the first year in which one country claimed all three European Individual titles—Men's, Ladies' and Junior. At Aachen David Broome scored with Sunsalve; at Deauville Pat Smythe won all three of her events, the first two with Scorchin' and the final one with Flanagan. Finally, Sheila Barnes won the Junior title at the C.H.I.O. meeting at Hickstead, Sussex.

Sheila Barnes on Miss N. R. Wheeler's Sola

ABOVE *Miss Waveney Hue-Williams and Ivanhoe moving to the starting point beyond Dunster Castle.* BELOW *Dunster Castle seen again above the dressage arena*

THE
BEAUTIFUL
SETTINGS
FOR
BRITAIN'S
HORSE
TRIALS

BURGHLEY
VENUE OF THE
1962 EUROPEAN
THREE-DAY EVENT
CHAMPIONSHIPS

With its undulating and beautifully established parkland, the Marquess of Exeter's magnificent Burghley House estate in Stamford, Lincolnshire, was a happy choice for the new site of the autumn trials formerly held at Harewood. The house itself is one of the finest examples of late Elizabethan architecture, and its beautiful facade made an elegant backdrop for the 1962 European Championships. 1961 saw the inaugural event at Burghley immediately winning many devotees, despite the solid course that confronted riders.

Miss Susan Fleet and The Gladiator

In the dressage ring—Ireland's Captain Harry Freeman Jackson and the great St Finbarr

The undulating park setting, with a romantic aspect of Burghley House in the middle distance

*Individual European Champions for 1962—
Capt. James Templar and his mount M'Lord
Connolly*

*English rain went unheeded by members of the
Russian contingent, on their way to a convincing
win in the team event. Preparing for the Roads
and Tracks phase—Rumb, mount of the Russian
Olympic rider, Boris Konjkov*

QUIET TRAINING BEHIND THE SCENES

Good public performances are like an iceberg—nine-tenths of the effort is never observed publicly. For weeks and months there are the painstaking training sessions, the interminable periods of exercise and the moments of doubt when minor or major setbacks crowd in and sow the seeds of doubt concerning the ultimate success of a particular venture. One's heart must be well and truly wedded to the job.

In the eminently suitable grounds at Castletown, County Kildare, the horses of the Conolly-Carew family are worked. LEFT *The Hon. Diana Conolly-Carew with Barrymore in front of Castletown House, one of Ireland's most superb Georgian edifices*

SOME TITLE WINNERS FROM THE 1961 HORSE OF THE YEAR SHOW AT WEMBLEY

ABOVE *Hunter of the Year: Swagger*

LEFT *Pony of the Year: Second Thoughts*

BELOW *Combined Training: Merely-a-Monarch*

Desert Storm—certainly one of the most brilliant hacks ever seen in the English show ring, and deservedly an immense favourite with the crowds. Owned by Miss Angela Stubbings, and trained and ridden by Miss Jennie Bullen, Desert Storm is the only hack to have won the Winston Churchill Challenge for the Supreme Riding Horse at the Royal International Horse Show on more than one occasion. With her usual eye-catching élan, Desert Storm closed her hack career with the title Hack of the Year for 1961 at Wembley. With the elegant and talented Miss Bullen to guide her, the mare is now making a new name for herself in dressage.

LEADING BRITISH HORSE TRIALS COMBINATION FOR 1961

Michael Bullen on Col. and Mrs V. D. S. Williams' Sea Breeze

Sea Breeze parades past Her Majesty the Queen in the stands at Badminton

AN
IMPRESSIVE
BADMINTON
WINNER

In the autumn of 1961 Anneli Drummond Hay and Merely-a-Monarch trounced the field in the Burghley Three-Day Event, and they started as the favourites for the Badminton Event of the following spring. Confidence in the pair was fully justified. With the ruling against women in the Olympic Three-Day Events still in force at that stage, Miss Drummond Hay diverted her outstanding horse's energies to pure showjumping and they made an auspicious beginning, representing their country within the year. At the end of the 1962 season, Mr Robert Hanson purchased Merely-a-Monarch as an addition to his 'string,' with Miss Drummond Hay continuing to partner the horse she brought to such prominence. The following year, the partnership came into its own in the showjumping sphere and early in the season was able to clinch Britain's win in the Nations Cup at the Rome Show with two clear rounds. Despite his thoroughbred hunter lines, Monarch's grandmother was in fact a Fell pony. In the stable, he is a horse of enormous and pleasant personality.

TOP *Merely-a-Monarch and Miss Drummond Hay open up a decisive lead in the Dressage phase at Badminton* . . .

CENTRE . . . *to be followed by a faultless Cross Country performance on the second day*

RIGHT *In the Showjumping phase, they maintain their lead with only one fence down*

LEFT *Part of the huge crowd which surges around the whole of the vast Badminton estate following the Cross Country route*

WAYS ACROSS WATER . . .

LEFT *Lt. Jeremy Smith-Bingham and By Golly*

RIGHT *Major Darley and Carrigtwohill give a wide berth to this stream*

SHOWJUMPING AT ASCOT

In its four years of existence, the Duchess of Norfolk's Ascot Jumping Show became something of a mecca for showjumping enthusiasts, not only for its judicial timing as an early seasonal pipe-opener, but also for its painstaking organization and willingness to cater for every grade of competitor. Three rings, and a dressage arena, functioned continually in the gracious setting of the racecourse, and the fantastic number of entries must surely have constituted a world record in their time.

In the running of the show, the Duchess has always been aided by her four daughters, and enthusiasts agree that no fixture has operated more satisfactorily. With the racecourse authorities' 1962 announcement of an increased use of the course in future years, it seemed that the last had been seen of this fine show, but so popular had it become that the Duchess of Norfolk was presented with a large petition begging her to organize the show on a different site.

There was no despondency evident at the last Ascot show of 1962, when interesting courses and magnificent prizes provoked four days of exceptional competition. ABOVE: The Duke and Duchess of Norfolk congratulate David Broome after his winning of a motor-car prize. With Wildfire III, David Broome had a remarkable week of good fortune.

Miss Ann Townsend on Bandit IV

Harvey Smith with .his non-chalent grey warrior Warpaint

ASCOT'S SETTING

added to the charm of the showjumping fixture and certainly some of the amenities could hardly have been bettered. Here, Miss Pat Smythe poses with Scorchin' and Bayridge for two informal photographic studies by the Ascot stables

SUNSALVE

This great, authentic star of showjumping died two months after this photograph was taken. A heart-attack cut him down as a twelve-year-old in the midst of a career which began and ended under the guidance of his owner's daughter—Mrs Elizabeth Anderson Slinn. She it was who had the responsibility of the big chesnut's early preparation for the show ring, and she demonstrated remarkable patience and tact in coping with the horse's highly-strung disposition, which manifested itself once a show ring was in sight. The horse adored jumping, but had scant regard for the niceties of pace and control. For him, action was the essence of the day. With the understandable reluctance to risk giving him a free head in his younger days, Sunsalve learned to place almost total reliance on the strength of his hind-quarters—a phenomenal power-house that obviated any necessity to bascule properly. With all these problems, Elizabeth Anderson, as she then was, managed to steer many courses to victory on her adored mount, including a renowned 1957 triumph in the Queen Elizabeth II Cup—the coveted supreme award for lady riders.

Sunsalve's liaison with David Broome for the 1960 Olympic Games year soon made headlines when the young rider scored in the male rider's supreme trophy, the King George V Gold Cup—Sunsalve thus becoming the only horse to clinch both titles. Their endeavours at Rome and Aachen in 1960 and 1961 are common knowledge. Mrs Slinn was just feeling her way into a renewed partnership with Sunsalve when the horse died. When other horses are forgotten, it will be Sunsalve's unquenchable primitive majesty in action that will always remain in the memory of those who watched him. It was a Frenchman watching Sunsalve on one of his days of international glory who murmured incredulously: "Ce n'est pas un cheval; c'est une gazelle!" He spoke for many.

SOME LEADING HANDS

"... Let this pressure of the hand say to thee
what is inexpressible."

GOETHE, *Faust*

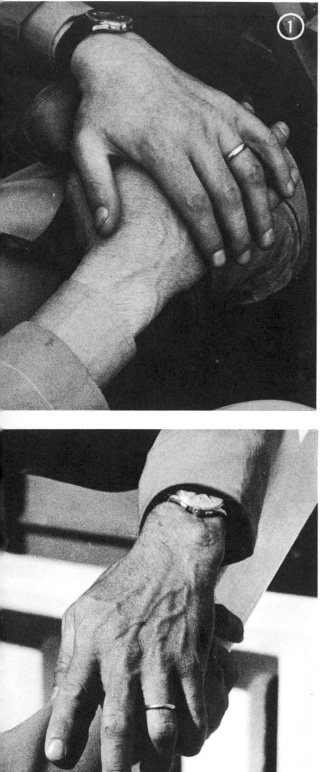

...but not a watchmaker's advertisement

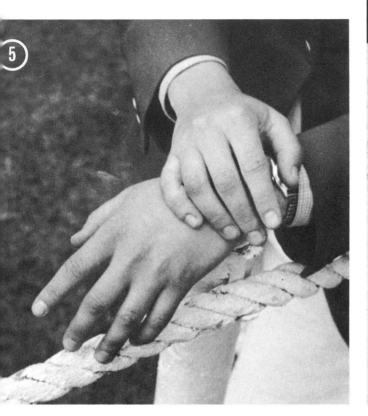

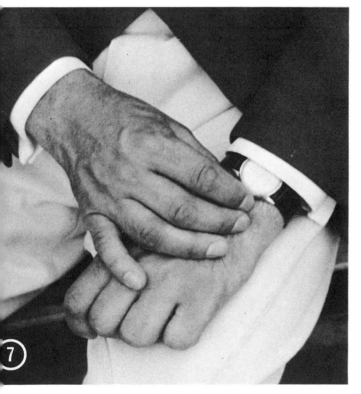

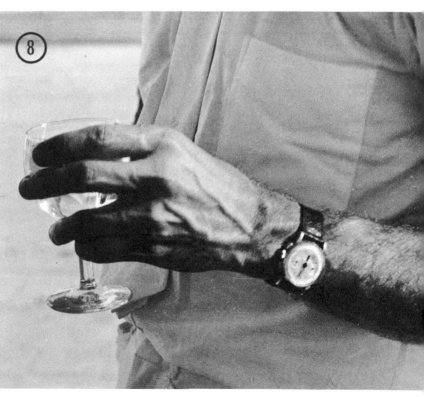

BRITISH JUMPING DERBY

All England Jumping Course, Hickstead, Sussex

Miss Kathy Kusner (U.S.A.) and High Noon on the Hickstead Bank

Hickstead's originator Douglas Bunn garlands Flanagan with the oak leaves of victory

With the running of the second British Jumping Derby at Hickstead in 1962, the meeting was firmly established as one of the 'prestige' events of the showjumping calendar. On this occasion, the fixture drew a strongly diverse field, with leading riders from Ireland, America and Germany competing against the national riders. From the whole competition only two riders emerged clear over the lengthy course of sixteen thought-provoking obstacles. In a thrilling jump-off, Pat Smythe emerged the winner with another faultless performance with Flanagan.

Despite the sunshine, Frank Chapot (U.S.A.) and San Lucas flying a 'mud tail.'

Dorian Williams, briefly in front of the television cameras for an introduction

Mrs Robert Hall and Conversano Caprice, Dressage Derby
winner

DIVERSION HICKSTEAD →

William Steinkraus (U.S.A.) and Sinjon winning the Derby Trial Stakes

LEFT *Second to Pat Smythe in the Derby,
Ireland's Tommy Wade and Dundrum*

BELOW *Mary Mairs and Vestryman (U.S.A.)
viewed from the Hickstead Club House veranda*

David Broome and Grand
Manan reaching for the open
water

Ask visiting international riders what it is that they remember about London's White City Stadium and the conversation will surely turn to the view from the Team tables in the Restaurant. The aspect never fails to intrigue. One can dine in more than adequate comfort and need barely raise one's eyes from the plate to observe all activity in the arena below. There is never the nagging doubt that one is missing a vital moment; the coffee can be finished in peace. From these heights, riders see their team mates' performances mapped out in the arena with awesome clarity—errors of judgment announce themselves in advance with terrible obviousness when viewed from such a position.

Lt. Campion of Ireland in silhouette

Waiting for the year's claimants—the Royal International Horse Show's two supreme awards for riders: the King George V Gold Cup (as the men's trophy is known) and the Queen Elizabeth II Cup for Lady Riders. The King George V trophy of St George is of exquisite workmanship. Won by Lt. Bettoni of Italy in 1939, the challenge trophy was not heard of again until the end of the war, when it was recognized amidst other loot buried in the rubble of an Italian village. Since then, the high insurance fee has meant that few riders have bothered to take it out of the country. Originally won outright by the then Lt.-Col. Jack Talbot-Ponsonby, the trophy was re-presented by him for perpetual competition. Col. Harry Llewellyn and Major Piero d'Inzeo have since emulated Col. Talbot-Ponsonby in winning it three times.

A Russian post-mortem

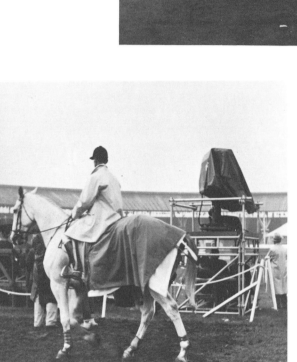

A
DAMP
SEQUENCE
OF
EVENTS — WHITE CITY
1962

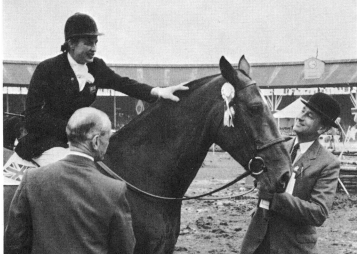

A BRIGHT
SEQUENCE
OF EVENTS

After a suitably affectionate form of congratulation from former colleague Harry Llewellyn, Pat Smythe returned with Flanagan to receive both the points prizes—the Saddle of Honour and the Loriners' Cup. Leaving the arena she was lost to sight in a flurry of eager fans. In the background stood Flanagan's proud owner, Mr Robert Hanson

No other arena in the world is as tense as London's when showjumping's First Lady is competing in an international final. Pat and Scorchin' won their second *Daily Mail* championship together in 1962; there had already been an earlier double with the renowned Prince Hal, making four *Daily Mail* Gold Cups in all which Miss Smythe has claimed. Only one other rider has won the cup even twice.

EUROPEAN MEN'S CHAMPION 1962

Britain repeated her record of the previous year when she again annexed all three European titles for 1962—Men's, Ladies' and Junior. The Men's Championship took place at the Royal International Horse Show during an atrociously wet week. The show committee departed from normal procedure in having three qualifying rounds whose points were not accumulative; the finalists had to risk all in the fourth competition. With commendable skill, Yorkshire's David Barker emerged ahead of his rivals as the leader on points after the three qualifying rounds. He had gained this position with Franco, his 1960 Olympic mount, but was faced with the problem of declaring which

Mister Softee

of his two mounts he would ride in the Final—a two-round competition. He chose the brilliant and level-headed Mister Softee, a mount which had first set the critics talking the previous season. The confidence was justified. Having gone clear in the first round, David Barker began his second round with the knowledge that to escape a jump-off he must have no more than one fence down. Three fences from home a red and white rail fell to an accompanying gasp from the huge crowd, but the twenty-six-year-old rider continued safely and the cheers broke out for a richly deserved victory. Hans Günter Winkler and Piero d'Inzeo were second equal with eight faults apiece. During the playing of the National Anthem (LEFT) Show Director Colonel Ansell, could be seen looking justifiably pleased with the turn of events. David Barker and Mister Softee ended the 1962 season with a successful private visit across the Atlantic, winning the Puissance Championship in Washington and the Grand Prix of New York. Mr John Massarella's horse had already been in winning form at the Horse of the Year Show immediately prior to leaving for the States, and he returned a worthy ambassador.

Franco

THE
DE NEMETHY
TOUCH

Can a leading trainer impart a widely recognized style to his team riders? To the riders themselves this idea might seem a stupid generalization, and of course there must be the personal idiosyncracies of a great rider such as Steinkraus, but nevertheless to an onlooker Bertalan de Nemethy's American team displays this unity of style to a marked degree. The elegance and precision of the team has been the cynosure of all eyes. Study these pictures.

TOP *Mary Mairs*

LEFT CENTRE *Hugh Wiley*

LEFT *Kathy Kusner*

176

George Morris

Bill Steinkraus

A U.S.E.T. Conference:

"Hey?"

"What's the matter?"

"We've got to salute."

"Salute? We did it over the other side."

"Yeah, but we've got to do it again."

"Where to?"

"Up there!"

"O.K. One, two, three . . ."

Frank Chapot

Bill Robertson

THE LAUGHTER IS ALWAYS BEHIND ME
Thoughts on photographing horses

If there *is* any laughter, it usually *does* come from behind. Particularly when I am manoeuvring for a shot. It has been explained to me that there is some reason for the suppressed giggles; that I do look rather absurd—more absurd—when I am trying to take photographs. Many people don't appreciate the degree of exactness demanded by horse photography. Like ballet dancing, the margin of acceptability for a movement or angle is slight indeed; the scorn of experts will be poured on photographs that many might consider adequate. 'Interesting' shots are particularly suspect. One must certainly throw dignity to the winds in pursuit of one's subject. It is no use standing elegantly detached at full height, rooted to the ground in a statuesque pose with camera to eye; the result is likely to be one of those embarrassingly awful shots which the evening newspapers sometimes use to fill an odd space on uneventful spring mornings (evening newspapers always seem to come out indecently early in the morning). The caption is often something like: 'A real horselaugh,' or 'Straight from the horse's mouth,' foreshortening having produced that terrifyingly enormous head—sometimes with lips curled back revealing a mouth full of teeth like piano keys—suspended magically on a neck the width of an average broom handle, trailing away to a midget and emaciated body disappearing into the soft focus. It is all so terribly easy.

The problems only begin when one tries to produce a photo that will not provoke too many comments like: "How could they possibly have given the championship to a bean-bag like that!" The champion's finer points have *all* got to be readily apparent in the photograph, hence the agitated contortions as one ducks and twists after a fractious animal, trying to maintain the magical position —not too high, not too low, not too near—which will prevent the subject coming out like a coroner's exhibit. There is the agonizing wait for that brief moment when, if luck and patience will have it, the ears, swishing tail, recalcitrant sunlight, confusing background and photographer's focal distance all coincide. How many times I have danced futile attendance on a bad-tempered horse (and/or rider) only to discover after twenty minutes capering that when the moment came I had failed to trigger the camera! I am the true amateur.

When moving into the fray in some foreign surroundings with my small and relatively antiquated Voigtlander 66 clutched casually in one hand, my sense of nakedness increases as other professional photographers glance around with ill-concealed amazement—almost contempt. "Who does he think he is?" their looks say. "Coming here with his auntie's camera. What a waste of time! Bet he pinched his Press Pass." Then they smile indulgently. They can afford to be helpful. They are not always so indulgent when they discover have I sneaked the best positions. One sometimes needs sharp elbows when not mixing with the 'regulars' that one knows. But there are advantages in being so bereft of 'professional' equipment. Ladies on the sideline are usually more than helpful, explaining such snags as distance and light and when I ought to press the trigger, as I squat in front of them.

'Panning' usually foxes them. "My dear, I'm afraid you will have blurred that one!" I have to pan my camera (to the uninitiated that means swinging the camera with the moving object), owing to the fact that I am limited to a top speed of 1/500th of a second. At fairly close quarters one hasn't a hope of achieving clarity with a moving horse and rider unless one perfects this 'golfing' swing. I think it adds to the interest of a picture, but sometimes as I crouch near a jump I feel a tinge of envy for the big boys sitting comfortably back near the railings, secure behind their bazooka lenses that obtain those pin-sharp studies of horses' shoe nails with such terrifying ease. When the inevitable day dawns and I receive my baptismal quota of blame and abuse from an enraged rider, then I think I shall take up bird photography—or maybe take up serious riding again. It would be fun to look down on the ranks so recently deserted.

Indoor shows such as Wembley's Horse of the Year usually have some form of individual equestrian display as a highlight for each performance. One popular and exotic figure has been the rejoneador Don Angel Peralta of Spain, whose Andalusian horses prove the veracity of the paintings by Velazquez. Seen here, caught between the horns of pursuing spotlights, Peralta demonstrates the agitated intricacies that save him and his partner from injury in the bullring

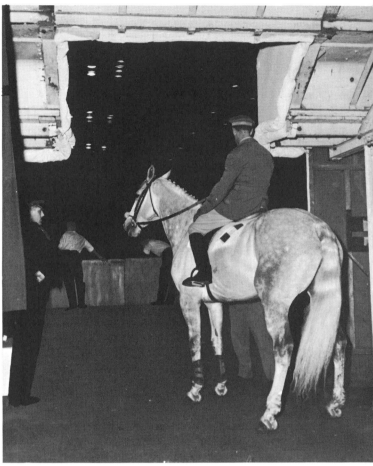

Major Piero d'Inzeo waits his turn beneath the reverberating structure of a packed house

A brotherly address from John Kidd to his sister Jane

THE SUBTLE MAGIC
OF INDOOR SHOWS

Atmosphere—sometimes thick atmosphere—is a quality of concentrated indoor shows. When the great Cavalcade takes place at Wembley, and the nostalgic Salute to the Horse is read, the arena contains horse-flesh of inestimable value and fame. 1962 saw the Guest of Honour spotlight centred on the jaunty figure of Mandarin, hero *par excellence* of the Steeplechasing world.

GREEN PLACES

Showgrounds have their distinct characteristics as do the countries they are a part of, but it is fair to say that two or three will stick in the memories of riders when other venues are long forgotten. Atmosphere can make uncompromisingly ugly metropolitan centres like London's White City seem strangely evocative; certainly the view from the Team tables in the Restaurant is unlike anywhere else. There is an Olympian feeling in being able to lift one's eyes from clean napery and adequate food and wine to the diminutive occurrences in the ring below, where events are mapped out on the arena like a game on green baize, and every false move by horse or rider is somehow foreseeable long before it happens.

If Aachen's green galloping sward is but a few minutes' taxi ride from one's hotel, so too, is Barcelona's Real Club de Polo—perhaps a bit longer, for the Generalissimo Franco Avenue seems never ending and one is lulled by the warm dry air and singing cicadas long before the unobtrusive entrance is reached. Once inside, the lavishness is startling, as are most of the haunts of Spain's wealthy. Plentiful labour sees to it that the clipped hedges are immaculately trimmed and washed of dust, framing the distant views of the city lying far below, with its glittering arc curving off into the haze. The casual atmosphere is all-pervading; the beautiful women emerge like rare butterflies to promenade in the late afternoon, secure in the knowledge that their equally impeccably garbed children have watchful nannies lurking, ready to conjure up a new outfit of clothes the moment their ebullient and irrepressible charges gather a trace of dust or dirt during their rampaging. In the background can be heard the plonk of tennis balls; the occasional splash from a diver in the swimming pool. Horses seem almost an afterthought as one or two riders stroll about the arena trailing small dogs on jewelled leads, letting the dogs inspect the jumps but paying little attention themselves to the obstacles they must soon negotiate. Before events get under way, the sky will have taken on the deep, honey-coloured glow of late afternoon, and screaming swallows will scythe above the crenellated skyline of the Military Headquarters brooding above this oasis.

Madrid, too, has more than a casual air of luxury about it where horse interests are concerned, with the remarkable settings of the Club de Campo nestling below the terracotta-coloured backdrop of the city buildings on the brow of the hill. Trimmed and decked with constantly watered greenery, the spacious setting is not only costly but imaginative. The stands themselves have a cool elegance of design, though without a hired cushion, the marble seating can be *too* cool when waning autumn comes around. All is leisure, social courtesies, bookmakers' tickets and the aromatic drift of Havana cigars.

Driving from Dublin Airport through the ravaged but still beautiful remains of Georgian back streets, with their shattered fanlights, dark and pocked like so many mouths full of bad teeth, one is ill-prepared for the luxuriant greenness and trim—almost prim—beauty of Ball's Bridge Showground. The colour of the turf intoxicates without leaving after-effects. Everything is light and freshness, with the constantly changing sky reflecting seagulls and intense blue in the fast-drying puddles of this rare demesne. If it is difficult to warm up a horse properly in the 'pocket' of Ball's Bridge Showground, it is certainly not difficult to take good pictures of them once they are in the flower-skirted ring. The atmosphere is conducive; nobody harries one. There is freedom to conduct oneself sensibly and where one sees fit. The jumps are always beautiful and varied; the light always producing a quality of stage management. The only distractions are the hilarious running comments from one's friends in the grandstands. They see nothing wrong in calling out from a considerable distance that your appearance "after last night" is little short of amazing. And the embarrassing thing is that they are always so right.

185

In an exciting series of competitions in Madrid, Pat Smythe concluded a truly memorable 1962 season by retaining her European Ladies' Showjumping Championship title. Flanagan was the object of some concern after an injury to a hock during air transport, but *he* seemed unconcerned, and finally appeared sound for the vital competitions. Second in the championship was Mrs Helga Köhler of Germany and third was Spain's Senora Paula Elizalde de Goyoaga.

THE CLUB DE CAMPO

Madrid's lavish club on the outskirts of the city is an establishment of great beauty and comfort. The arena is all that could be desired, while the adjoining training ground has such a comprehensive collection of jumps that it defies counting. The obstacles are built to specifications gathered from all over the world, and visitors tend to leave this beautifully appointed domain with distinct inferiority complexes.

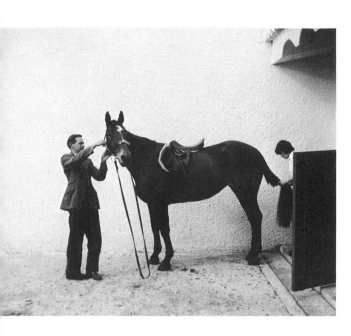

*On this occasion Brian Crago
lends a hand with one of his
wife's horses*

*Jean Harper's Ignatius
surrenders his studs*

HOMAGE
TO THE GROOMS

*That faithful band that
makes it all possible*

*Frank Leach, U.S.E.T.,
in full flight*

189

RIDERS AND OWNERS

Italic page numbers refer to illustrations

William

Susan Cohen

Amel. Drummond

Mike Ball

Sarah Howard

Dawn Wofford

Adrian White

Derek Allhusen

Lawrence R. Morgan

A. E. Hill

Raimondo d'Inzeo

Hugh Wiley

Pat Moss.

Norman Bunn

Bob Grayson

Frank Chapot

A. Queralow

Douglas Bunn

Renata Freitag

Kathy Kusner